FROM TRAUMA TO *Tranquility*

FROM TRAUMA TO *Tranquility*

A Guide to Inner Peace

GILLIAN PADGETT

SWS
PUBLISHING

Published in 2018.

SWS Publishing, Vernon, British Columbia V1T 9M9, Canada

ISBN: 978-0-9953061-2-7—Paperback edition
ISBN: 978-0-9953061-3-4—E-book
1. Trauma 2. Stress 3. Stress Management 4. Holistic Health
5. Self-Help

National Library of Canada Cataloguing in Publication Data: A cataloguing record for this book that includes the US Library of Congress classification number, the Library of Congress call number, and the Dewey Decimal cataloguing code is available from the National Library of Canada. The complete cataloguing record can be obtained from the National Library's online database at: www.nlc-bnc.ca/amicus/index-e.html.

Book Design by Constellation Book Services
Diagram Images: ShutterstockAnna Rassadnikova
Graphics and content in appendices used by permission
Photography: www.keylightphotography.ca

Disclaimer: This book is not intended as an alternative to professional medical advice. The reader should consult a healthcare professional in all matters related to physical, mental, emotional and spiritual well-being, particularly with respect to any symptoms causing concern that might require diagnosis and medical attention.

This book is dedicated to

YOU

Also by Gillian Padgett

Let Stress Heal Your Life:
Uncover Your Amazing Capacity to Thrive

Stress Wisdom: The Holistic Approach to Stress

Please visit
www.stresswisdomsolutions.com
www.stresswisdomsolutions.com/blog

Contents

To ensure absolute confidentiality, the names and descriptions of the people whose experiences are discussed in this book have been changed to protect their identities.

Preface

My purpose in writing this book is to help you understand some of the causes, stages and symptoms of stress and trauma so that you will be able to recognize them yourself. I also offer a selection of practical strategies and tools to help you and your loved ones along the journey of recovery. This understanding and information can relieve fear, panic and a sense of helplessness; reduce overwhelm and stress; and facilitate and speed the ability to heal.

When you recognize what's going on with you and have steps to follow, you can begin to take action. As you do so, you will trigger two powerful forces:

- **The placebo effect**, which in scientific studies has been shown to be effective for healing;
- **The mind**, which research shows influences our energy, our well-being and our healing.

The book covers the following information:

Chapter 1. Trauma Simplified provides insight into trauma.

Chapter 2. Stage 1: Impact—What to Do Immediately after Trauma Hits discusses three steps that will help you begin to shift from trauma to well-being, details five strategies for getting sufficient sleep and provides three simple guidelines to help you create a support system.

Chapter 3. Stage 2: Recovery helps to remove fear by providing information on physical, mental and emotional reactions to trauma and stress and offering tips and strategies so you can move from trauma to recovery as easily as possible. This chapter also provides information on different ways we can be traumatized. For example, the trauma of being in a car accident is very different from the trauma of losing a partner in a car accident, although the *initial impact* of trauma in both cases could be similar.

Chapter 4. Stage 3: Change, Wisdom and Peace provides appropriate techniques and strategies to use at any time to assess how you are within your mind, body, emotions and spirit and to help you move towards well-being.

We are invariably changed by trauma. Initially we may be angry or resentful. We may think, "Why did this happen to me?" Ultimately, however, we are likely to become kinder and more compassionate with ourselves and others.

My greatest wish is that this book will help you understand and overcome trauma and move towards inner peace and tranquility.

Introduction

We are able to do everything in our power to create lives for ourselves that are enriching and nourishing on a daily basis. We can have the knowledge and skills to handle everyday stresses with competence and ease. To this end, I have things pretty well set up.

My home is in the middle of a provincial park, on a mountain in British Columbia, Canada. I thrive in nature and beauty and am surrounded by magnificent views and wildlife. Wherever I walk, the smells, sights and sounds are home to my heart. Every drive in my car nourishes my soul.

Except one.

It was a particularly grey morning following a heavy snowfall. The road was icy and had just been gritted. My car was fitted with studded tires and I wasn't driving fast. I had driven this particular road thousands of times in all weathers and I felt safe. I'd just dropped my dog off for her quarterly groom and was looking forward to a cup of coffee when I arrived home.

In the blink of an eye, my car careened across the road and over a ditch. It made grinding and scraping sounds and suddenly stopped with a very loud bang as it crashed into the mountainside. Then silence.

Staring through the windscreen as I hurtled towards the mountain, I wondered, "Is this it?" It wasn't. After the impact, I was still alive. Someone kindly stopped, helped me out of the car and drove me the rest of the way home.

My car had buckled and was a total write-off. Miraculously, I was only bruised, although severely so. Nonetheless, the accident was traumatizing, and over the coming weeks, I gently moved through shock and trauma towards recovery and healing. I put into practice what I have taught my clients over the years to help them cope with challenge, stress and trauma.

What I learnt from this experience is that we can't prepare for trauma ahead of time in quite the same way that we can for stress. Trauma arises from unexpected and uncontrollable events and affects us deeply. It plummets us into shock, flashbacks and a variety of reactions, as well as taking us through some of the more common stress responses.

Following the accident, I observed myself and my reactions, many of which I had never experienced before. I was in a great deal of pain, so moving was extremely uncomfortable. I couldn't hold down food or water to begin with and wasn't hungry or thirsty anyway. As time passed, I was in awe of the ever-changing display of multi-colored bruises.

For three weeks I slept a large portion of the time. Sleep is what my body normally demands to repair, readjust and heal. When I wasn't sleeping, I began to review other traumas in my life. There were quite a few, including separation from my parents at an early age, divorce, deaths in the family and the murder of a close friend. None of those events were in my control; the only power I had was how I responded. Whether or not I consciously worked on myself to prevent lasting damage made a significant difference to how long the effects of these painful events stayed with me.

Generally, I have found that increased compassion and kindness and a deeper understanding of themselves are indicators that my clients have moved through trauma satisfactorily. They may still feel some mental, emotional or physical pain, but they don't bathe in toxic anger, hatred, resentment or a desire for revenge. Nor do they sit in immune-suppressing victimhood, depression or hopelessness.

As a therapist who has specialized in stress for more than twenty-five years, I have supported many clients as they have made astonishing recoveries from trauma, stress and life's hard knocks, and I have lived through my own share of them. As with the car accident, many of my experiences have grounded theory into personal reality and added to my skill set, which has helped me to help others from a place of deeper understanding.

I've always enjoyed and been interested in people. When I was working as an interior designer in London, England, I found that after discussing renovations, color, furniture and fabrics with my clients, I took on another role that I loved. I became the holder of confidences and dreams.

In retrospect, it is not at all surprising that my career shifted and I became a hypnotherapist and psychotherapist, a profession in which I was able to not only hold confidences and dreams but also help people overcome their problems.

Life leads us, not the other way around—at least, that is how it has happened with me. Following the murder of my best friend and then witnessing the devastation of her family, I chose to take trainings in the United Kingdom to work with victims of crime and families of murder victims. This led me to study stress and well-being from as many perspectives as I could find. I sought to understand how stress affects the brain, mind, body, emotions and spirit and discovered causes, remedies and solutions within areas of specialty as varied as nutrition, psycho-neuroimmunology, spiritual healing and energy medicine. I continue to study and learn. Helping people master stress and overcome trauma has become the focus of my work.

We now know that poorly managed stress is the foundation of most illnesses. This is reason enough to want to better understand stress and trauma so that we can competently nourish and nurture ourselves in mind, body, emotions and spirit and be able to handle whatever comes our way on our journey through life.

From Trauma to Tranquility provides practical, effective strategies, tips and techniques for you to implement in your own way and at your own pace. They help to remove shock, fear and stress arising from trauma. The exercises will help you develop the skills to detect imbalance and identify the best steps to take to return to balance, inner peace and tranquility.

CHAPTER 1
Trauma Simplified

Trauma is the result of a deeply distressing and disturbing experience, causing serious physical, mental or emotional injury. It creates shock and fear and affects our sense of safety, control and trust.

Stress, on the other hand, is frequently the result of pressure, causing mental, emotional and physical tension. Stress can slowly sneak up and accumulate over time and harm health and well-being.

Situations such as caring for a sick child, taking exams, pressure at work or being in a bad relationship are stressful and require coping strategies, but they are unlikely to be traumatizing. On the other hand, escaping a house fire or having a classmate shot and killed in front of you at school can cause deep shock and neurological and physiological impact, and can trigger repetitive reactions.

Put simply, the difference between stress and trauma can be as stark as the difference between a pebble and a boulder landing on your foot while you're sitting on a park bench admiring a waterfall. Although both would be unexpected, the falling pebble may cause slight stress from surprise, yet it would not even cause bruising and would be quickly forgotten. On the other hand, the boulder could smash bones, damage nerves and cause physical pain. The injuries could take a long time to heal, and the impact of the event could create a sense of fear and even cause phobias or panic attacks.

Traumatic Events

Traumatic events include having an accident of any sort, being a victim of crime, experiencing the death of a loved one, living through a natural disaster, being diagnosed with a serious illness or having surgery. They also include being tortured, dealing with war, being abused as a child, being abandoned, suffering from bereavement, going through a divorce or suffering emotional abuse or neglect. Those who suffer near drowning, battery or being the victim of violence experience traumatic events. There are many, many other ways to be traumatized, but this list gives a broad picture.

Witnessing something shocking can also be traumatizing; for example, a child seeing a parent being attacked, an emergency responder arriving at the scene of an accident and even watching a shocking event on television.

Some Reactions and Feelings Related to Trauma

Denial is a common reaction after one has experienced trauma. After my car accident, I arranged for the car to be towed, handled the insurance claim, cleaned the house and saw clients, despite the fact that I was in a great deal of pain. Only after all those tasks were done did I recognize the full impact of what had happened to me; I felt full-blown shock and fear—but very lucky. It was much later in my healing process that I felt truly grateful that my car had crossed the road and hit the mountain rather than slipping over the edge on the side I was driving. As immediately after the accident, again I had to work through feeling out of control, unsafe and afraid.

The stress response (see appendix 1) is triggered by fear and activates a variety of life-saving physiological reactions so that we can instantly escape danger. At some point our emotions are affected and we may feel afraid, angry, enraged, helpless, hopeless, overwhelmed or tearful. In addition, memory, concentration and focus as well as other mental skills can be affected, as can the all-important ability to sleep.

Post-Traumatic Stress Disorder

Following trauma, extreme reactions can be triggered by sights, sounds, touch, tastes, smells, thought processes, emotions and how we feel physically. All of these reactions can subconsciously loop back to the point of trauma.

Jo used to visit his father once a week. He would buy groceries and then share a meal and chat with him. On his last visit, his father wasn't watching television or sitting in his chair in the living room. He didn't reply when called. Jo went upstairs and found his father dead in his bed. Immediately afterwards, Jo handled the funeral and cleared his father's home. But the shock had been immense and he kept seeing images of his father dead. He felt guilty and sad, couldn't sleep properly and regretted never having said goodbye. Jo suffered from the trauma of his father's death long after the event.

Some responses to trauma, including flashbacks, can be frightening. The night of my car accident, every time I closed my eyes I had flashbacks. I could hear, see and feel myself inside my car as it was propelled against the mountainside. As it was impossible to sleep, I spent the entire night with all the lights on in my home, working to break the stress response and rewire my brain to stop the flashbacks. The next night, I was able to sleep.

War veterans may react unexpectedly to sudden sounds, such as a car backfiring, which reconnect fear, feelings and memories related to a traumatic event they experienced. Having spent time on high alert in a war zone, when they are back in the civilian world, they may respond with extraordinary violence or emotion when they are startled, feel helpless or are challenged over something that seems unimportant or trivial to others. They often become afraid of their own feelings and reactions.

People often withdraw when they are unable to handle the symptoms of post-traumatic stress disorder. If they have participated in acts of war, they may also suffer from a deep sense of shame and guilt. Sleep can be elusive, their digestion and health suffer, and they may turn to medication, drugs or alcohol in an attempt to numb themselves.

In my book *Let Stress Heal Your Life,* I mention a client who had a full-blown panic attack that was triggered when he had a cup of tea. Normally he drank coffee, but on this particular afternoon he fancied tea. The taste of the tea made a direct neurological connection to the shock he experienced after he was rescued from a boating accident in which a friend had drowned. After being rescued my client was wrapped in blankets and given a cup of hot, sweet tea.

Who Experiences Trauma?

Most people experience traumatic events in their lives. If trauma hasn't yet crossed your path, you can fairly accurately assume that it may be just around the corner.

The same event can be experienced differently by different people. Many people can be in a traumatic situation, handle the trauma, remain untraumatized, recover from the shock and carry on, wiser and well, while others can experience the same event and suffer severe reactions to the trauma.

Then there are the "walking wounded," people who react inappropriately to circumstances and other people due to an unresolved imprint of trauma on their psyche. When they delve into their past, these people often discover a suppressed trauma, perhaps from childhood, that still holds an emotional and energetic charge for them. When the charge is defused or desensitized and the event is reviewed and its effects healed, they no longer react, become numb or are overly sensitive to events and people in their lives.

Research shows that childhood trauma negatively affects physical health in middle age and later. Whatever someone's age, it is well worthwhile to clear the traumas, past and present, and be able to move forward into a healthy future.

Losing one's home in a fire, miraculously surviving a brutal attack or being an emergency responder at Ground Zero on 9/11 would be traumatic to most people, yet seemingly insignificant events can be traumatic, too. Depending on one's personality and how quickly one is saved, being knocked over by a wave and nearly drowning as a young child could be frightening, traumatic and create a lasting fear of water. Or it could be considered exciting and treated as a joke.

Signs and Symptoms of Trauma

Immediately following a traumatic experience, we are likely to feel shocked, unsafe and afraid. In addition, we may feel afraid of the dark or of being alone or become forgetful, tearful or argumentative. We may be triggered into fear or other negative emotions by sights, sounds, smells and sensations; be unable to laugh, smile or find any joy in life; or blank out all memory related to the incident. We may be unable to be creative. We may feel very angry most of the time, have difficulty concentrating, have nightmares or problems sleeping, hide or retreat from the world or keep replaying the event in our minds. We may lose interest in life, talk incessantly and repetitively about the event, tremble, feel chilled to the bone, develop high blood pressure or have breathing difficulties. We may eat poorly, binge eat, be unable to eat at all or have stomach upsets or constipation. And we may feel hopeless and helpless.

We may also react to people or circumstances by people-pleasing, becoming aggressive, acting and feeling like a victim or falling into shallow sexual liaisons. We may start taking drugs or drinking alcohol to excess or be unable to emotionally connect with others.

These are just some of the ways people respond to trauma. We may have no reaction, one or more of these reactions or reactions that have not been mentioned.

Summary

Trauma arises from one or more events or situations that impact us negatively at a very deep level mentally, emotionally, physically and spiritually.

Invariably, traumatic events are outside our control and shock. Frequently they cause us to feel unsafe and afraid. We may be physically injured and have to cope with related pain. We may experience horrific emotional toll from either witnessing or being involved in something that had previously been unimaginable. Our lives may be changed forever if, for example, we have lost a loved one, or our home to fire, flood or disaster.

We may feel traumatized long after a traumatic event, reacting unexpectedly and seemingly inappropriately when triggered.

CHAPTER 2

Stage 1: Impact – What to Do Immediately after Trauma Hits

As an undercover cop, Dave loved everything about his job: the grounding routine and procedures mixed with adrenalin-inducing work in the underworld. He had had his share of challenging moments but had handled and recovered from them effortlessly. But after he was stabbed in his hand and arm, he found himself unable to cope with the trauma.

Following the incident, Dave had to have surgery. He healed well physically, although it took much longer than he expected. His doctor wouldn't sign him off to return to work or permit him to ride his motorbike, which was an essential part of his undercover work. He began to be afraid that he would end up in a desk job.

Dave hadn't been sleeping well, and his hands shook to the extent that it was almost impossible for him to write legibly. In addition, he seemed to be a bundle of nerves, jumping at the sound of a door shutting or a car backfiring. He looked tight and tense.

Before we discussed the details of the stabbing incident, Dave learnt steps to break the stress response: he learnt to breathe long, deep and low and to follow steps for progressive body relaxation. In addition, I gave him guidelines to create a safe place in his mind and to be able to sleep well.

Along with drinking enough water, eating well and applying tips on using his mind effectively, these were the only steps that Dave needed to fully recover and be allowed to return to work and drive his motorbike.

My understanding was that Dave was locked into the stress response—anxiety and fear—as he desperately tried to recover and return to the work he loved. He had been tense from the pain, afraid to relax and so increased his tension. Not being able to sleep had made matters far worse for him.

This chapter covers the steps that Dave followed. Very often they are all we need to get back on track. They are powerful and highly effective, and I give these steps to all my clients who are suffering from trauma and stress.

The stress response is designed to give us instant energy and power to fight or run from danger, and a vast number of changes occur in the brain, body, and limbs (see appendix 1). Immediately after danger, when we relax, the body's systems will naturally return to normal. However, instead of relaxing, all too often we replay the trauma in our minds over and over again. This retraumatizes, keeping our bodies on high alert ready for the next danger, and we are unable to relax or sleep well. This can cause problems such as those Dave experienced.

The First Three Steps to Shift from Trauma

Whenever we feel extreme fear, the brain triggers a multitude of reactions in the body (see appendices 1 and 2), which in turn affect the emotions and mind. If these stress responses are not quickly switched off, they can harm health and hinder recovery.

In addition to feeling afraid, most trauma victims also feel unsafe. A brilliant and highly effective formula to relieve tension and feel calm and safe is to flow from a breathing technique, to deep relaxation, to imagining being in a safe place. These techniques can also be effective when practiced individually.

There is an MP3 available on my website that you can download to follow these steps. It leads you through the breathing technique, deep relaxation and creating a safe place. You can access it here: www.stresswisdomsolutions.com/fromtraumatotranquility. You may find that listening to a recording of the scripts in your own voice is helpful. If you choose to do this, remember to read slowly and leave lots of gaps to allow your body and subconscious mind to process in their own way at their own speed and to deeply relax.

Once you have mastered this process, any time you need to feel extra comfort or safety, you will be able to breathe deeply and imagine that your body is relaxed and that you are in a safe place. Your body will follow your mind and become relaxed. You will also be able to breathe yourself calm in a traffic jam or while waiting for an interview or exam.

To create atmosphere, light a candle, play gentle music or use a diffuser to release your favorite relaxing essential oils. Then take the following steps to begin shifting from trauma.

BREATHING

Deep breathing is known to stabilize blood pressure, take in more oxygen, aid sleep, release toxins, improve blood flow and increase a feeling of calm.

- Sit, stand or lie as comfortably as you can, ideally with your spine straight.
- Inhale through your nose and exhale through your mouth (closing your mouth as you breathe in and opening it slightly as you breathe out).
- As you breathe in, imagine refreshing, energizing air reaching the lower part of your lungs. Your shoulders remain still and your stomach expands.
- As you breathe out, imagine your lungs releasing any stale air. Your shoulders remain still and your stomach moves in (towards your spine).
- Begin to create a slow, gentle rhythm as you breathe in and out.
- Focus on your breath throughout the process.
- Notice your body beginning to relax. This may be when you naturally take a deep breath.

Note: A variation for this breathing technique is to imagine breathing in calmness or safety with each in-breath and releasing fear and tension with each out-breath. Once you have mastered this easy, effortless, comfortable method of breathing, you can deepen and expand your breaths. To do so, count to four as you breathe in, hold for the count of four, breathe out to the count of four and hold for the count of four. Continue with this new rhythm, ensuring that it is comfortable and easy. If you feel dizzy, stop and return to the original simple method of breathing.

Affirmation: My breathing is slow,
deep and calming.

DEEP RELAXATION

Deep relaxation switches on disease-fighting genes, protects against pain, boosts immunity, improves heart health, relieves anxiety and eases digestive disorders such as irritable bowel syndrome.

Before you begin, ensure your body is a comfortable temperature. Have a blanket or socks close by, because often as we relax, our body temperature drops.

- Sit or lie down. Make sure you are comfortable.
- Continue to breathe easily and effortlessly.
- Become aware of your body.
- Become aware of the surface you are on.
- Imagine that you have the power to relax your muscles, smooth your skin and ease

tension as you slowly go through the deep relaxation process, taking as long as you like.

One of my favourite imaginings is of a drop of warm, golden oil dropping onto my skin. As it touches me, it relaxes my muscles, and healing energy sinks and spreads into my body, cells, organs and limbs.

Maybe you will enjoy imagining something you find calming, such as a sunbeam, touching, warming and relaxing your skin and muscles. Or imagine a feather, an angel or someone you love just above the surface of your body, or touching or holding your hand, spreading comfort and relaxation throughout your head, body and limbs.

The following is a script you can use for relaxation. Remember to read it slowly.

Become aware of your head and imagine that the muscles ease, release tension and feel more deeply relaxed around your scalp ... forehead ... eyes ... cheeks ... nose ... ears ... mouth ... tongue ... jaw ... releasing tension ... increasing comfort and ease.

Become aware of your neck, imagining that you are easing muscles, releasing tension in your neck

... throat ... shoulders ... back ... muscles on either side of your spine ... arms ... wrists ... hands ... fingers ... releasing tension ... increasing ease and comfort.

Become aware of your body, imagining that muscles release tension in your chest ... lungs ... stomach ... organs ... buttocks ... thighs ... knees ... calves and shins ... ankles ... feet ... toes ... releasing tension ... increasing ease and comfort.

Become aware of your whole body; notice if there are any areas of tension or discomfort. If there are, imagine them to be relaxing—becoming warmer or cooler, heavier or lighter, and more comfortable.

Perhaps you would like to feel even more relaxed or comfortable. If so, imagine that as you breathe you can gently become more comfortable, more relaxed.

Know that as you easily and gradually release tension ... and your body gently becomes more relaxed ... your mind also begins to relax ... your body is able to let go ... begin to heal ... and you can begin to feel more and more comfortable ... in every way.

Enjoy the sensation as long and as often as you wish.

Affirmation: I am comfortable and relaxed

CREATING A SAFE PLACE

Visualization reduces stress and limitation, aids creativity and supports mental health. As we use our minds to remember and create a sense of comfort and safety, our emotions and body respond by releasing tension and keeping the stress response at bay.

The Cave

Over the years I have created a number of special safe places for myself and my clients. One that I often retreat to in my mind is a beautiful, dry mountainside cave. The floor is covered in soft, sweet-smelling herbs and moss, and from the entrance there are wonderful views of the countryside below.

At the back of the cave is a tunnel leading to a pool of emerald water. The surface is dappled by sunlight.

The pool is filled by a gentle, soothing, musical waterfall, and the water is warmed by natural hot rocks way below. Written notes of unwanted memories and pain can be dropped down a narrow chute and onto the hot rocks to become smoke and ash. Anytime I take myself to this place, I feel calm.

A Beautiful, Calming Safe Place

Your safe place can be real or imagined. It is important that you involve all your senses in your imagining. Sense in your mind certain aspects of this place: colours, light and shade, objects; hear sounds; smell aromas; taste; and feel surface textures and so forth.

Here are the keys for creating your own beautiful, calming safe place:

- *Remember or create a place in your mind. Somewhere you feel very safe.*
- *Imagine yourself there in that place and feel how it is; a comfortable chair or bed, the feel of fabric, wood, water, a breeze or sunshine.*
- *What sounds can you hear? Birdsong, water, laughter, music, the wind, singing?*
- *Can you taste or smell anything?*
- *Maybe there are people you want to have there with you—a loving grandparent, your best*

friend, someone you felt safe with as a child or your teddy bear?

- *Enjoy the overall sense of safety, and remember to return there, to the place and feelings, whenever you wish.*

Here is another guide for creating a safe place. Follow the wording, or change the script to make your safe place a field, a room, a beach or wherever you can feel safe.

- *Be comfortable, breathe and relax.*
- *As you breathe gently ... allow your mind to wander and create a perfect place to feel comfortable, safe and at home.*
- *Stand in front of this place ... Is there a door? What colour is it? Imagine walking towards it.*
- *As you relax, imagine being there now - opening the door and stepping inside ...Where are you now?*
- *What can you see in front of and around you? ... What colours, items are there?*
- *Breathing easily and gently ... what can you smell? Most places have their very own unique smell.*
- *Now take yourself to your favourite room or*

place. Is there somewhere to sit, feel comfortable? ... And be there now?

- *Maybe you can see something that reminds you of a time when you felt loved, happy and safe.*
- *Feeling comfortable now, where do you feel that feeling of love ... happiness ... safety? In your heart? Your stomach? Your mind?*
- *Is there a window or a view? ... What can you see in your mind's eye?*
- *What can you hear?*
- *What do you want to remember of this place? ... And this feeling?*
- *Breathing gently ... with your body comfortable and relaxed ... return to the present moment now, bringing with you from that place some of the feelings of comfort, relaxation and safety—and return to your safe place whenever you wish.*

Affirmation: I am safe.

These three steps, breathing, deep relaxation and creating a safe place, are very powerful. They take your body, emotions and mind away from trauma and stress, even if only for a short while.

Check In

I suggest that you develop the habit of checking in with yourself regularly throughout the day. How are you feeling? Are you relaxed or tense? Stressed or at ease? If you feel tense or stressed, take yourself through the first three steps.

Develop the habit of going through the three steps at least three times a day—morning, midday and early evening—and maybe at bedtime, as well. You may find it helpful to do this more often immediately after experiencing trauma, and during the night to help you sleep.

As you practice this process, fluidly following one step after the other, you will gradually stretch and strengthen your mental, emotional and subconscious flexibility and resilience. Eventually you will be able to achieve a sense of inner calm in a matter of moments.

Affirmation: I am relaxed, calm and safe now.

Five Strategies to Sleep Well

It is not at all unusual for sleep to evade us shortly after a traumatic event. Our minds race, our bodies are tense or injured and we feel scared and on high alert for further danger. It is almost impossible to sleep when we are uptight and adrenalin is coursing through our bodies. And yet, restful sleep is essential to recover from trauma, stress and anything else that disturbs our equilibrium. During sleep, we process pain, put in order events from the day, and begin to heal.

Following are five strategies for sleeping well. Before you begin, remember to be patient with yourself as you take steps to return to sleeping naturally and healthily.

1. Create a regular bedtime. Plan to go to bed at the same time each night and get up at the same time in the morning to develop a rhythm to your sleep pattern. If you can't sleep after twenty or thirty minutes, get up and read or listen to gentle music. This will help to avoid associating your bed with struggling to sleep. Then go back to bed again. Don't panic if you can't sleep. You will soon be able to do so.
2. Eat or drink something nourishing half an hour before bedtime. Research shows that going to bed hungry can cause wakefulness and interfere with sleep.

3. Have a warm, relaxing bath before bedtime. Don't take a shower or bath with hot or cool water, as these can stimulate wakefulness. Add a few drops of lavender oil to the water to help relaxation if desired.
4. When you get to bed, follow the first three steps: breathing, deep relaxation and creating a safe place. If you have recorded the steps, play the recording, and follow the process over and over again. If you wake up in the night, repeat the process.
5. Cheat! Nap or even take sleeping pills for a while—ideally take natural, herbal and non-addictive sleeping pills. Monitor what you take, how you feel and how you sleep, and have professional guidance to come off any pills. Sleeping pills can interfere with the natural rhythm of sleep, be addictive and cause nightmares when we come off them. Generally, it is best to use them only for short-term support and avoid the complications of dependence on pills.

Affirmation: Sleep is 100 percent natural.
I can sleep soundly.

Three Simple Strategies

1. PEOPLE—SUPPORT FOR OURSELVES AND OTHERS

Each one of us is unique with respect to our history, background, beliefs, psychology and physiology. Trauma shocks us to the core and triggers a number of responses that are the result of a combination of these factors and the stress response. Thus, we process and express the effects of trauma differently, as is often seen within a family. The ways we process pain are connected to our coping skills. They have nothing to do with how much we love.

Find Support

Being stoic or heroic can hinder healing. Allow yourself to relax in the comfort of being cared for and supported for a while. If possible, find someone you trust to help with practicalities that are currently challenging or even overwhelming, such as shopping, cooking and running errands.

Find someone outside your close-knit circle to support you and be a calming presence. This should be a person who will be unconditionally accepting, treat your time together in confidence and allow you to cry, be angry or talk as you go through the natural healing stages following your trauma.

Be Kind

Remember to be kind and not rely on a parent or partner to support or carry your pain. They may barely be able to cope themselves. This can help keep the relationship alive if it was strong before the unthinkable occurred.

Statistics are frighteningly high for couples to separate following tragedy and trauma. Sharing love and loving memories with your partner can help you to stay connected.

2. DRINK WATER

Stress can cause us to sweat and urinate more than normal, have diarrhea, vomit, lose our appetite and become dehydrated. Sip water through the day, whenever you remember to. Add a little lemon juice if you don't like the taste of water. Add electrolytes (purchased from a pharmacy or health store) to replace some of the minerals you lose through fluid loss.

Avoid alcohol (it is a depressant) as well as sugary and caffeinated drinks. They all change brain and body chemistry. Drinking just one of any of them would more than likely cause no harm, but it would be wise to seek advice from your healthcare professional about this.

3. KEEP WARM

The stress response causes blood to go from the extremities to the muscles and heart (see appendix 1). Following shock and when we are stressed, our feet and hands may feel cold, and often our body can feel cold as well.

To get warm, add extra layers of bedding and clothing, cuddle up to a hot water bottle, warm your feet and hands in warm to hot water or soak in a warm to hot bath. You may find that your dog or cat comes and lies beside you. Mine hopped onto the bed and stayed beside me immediately after my accident and, as I recovered, they gradually went back to their normal sleeping spots.

Summary

These guidelines helped Dave, the undercover cop, immeasurably. He went from being uptight, on edge and barely able to write, to being relaxed, caring for himself and returning to work. We can all benefit from taking refreshing and relaxing moments and being able to spontaneously release symptoms of stress and trauma.

CHAPTER 3

Stage 2: Recovery

Recovery can be a natural process. When working with victims of crime and people who have had traumatic experiences, I always suggest that they begin by following the strategies in the previous chapter to break the stress response and allow natural healing to occur. I remind them that when people say they will never recover, those people are expressing their belief and not fact. Many, many people have recovered from all manner of things, including trauma.

The first three steps to shift from trauma to well-being provide an opportunity for healing to begin by gently easing tension. The next stages in recovery include moving through fear, and desensitizing traumatic memories and reactions, and handling stress and building resilience. They occur in no particular order but rather as issues arise that need attention. For some people, trauma seems to act like an earthquake or a hurricane, shattering their foundation and scattering all sense of order hither and thither. Recovery then becomes a matter of rearranging memory and balance as well as reassessing values and beliefs.

One purpose of this section is to help you to recognize some natural symptoms of stress and trauma and to remove unnecessary fear from an already stressful state. It is important to note that each of us is likely to feel some, but not all, of the symptoms of stress I have mentioned. The other purpose is to offer practical strategies and suggestions to gently return to balance.

Moving Through Fear

Although many traumatic events and tragedies happen in a matter of minutes or even seconds, survivors are often surprised by the long-lasting fallout.

I once watched a brave young student tearfully talk about the after-effects of a shooting at her school. She mentioned that she felt afraid all the time and couldn't even go to the bathroom alone. This reminded me of when our house was burgled. The point of entry and exit had been my eight-year-old son's bedroom window. For a long time afterwards he wouldn't go upstairs without Crispy, our large Briard dog. When he did go back to sleeping in his own room again, he had to have Crispy with him to feel safe.

The surprising, shocking and sometimes life-threatening nature of trauma can leave us feeling vulnerable. Realistically, we can't safeguard ourselves from every possible eventuality in the future. While the fear, trauma and stress responses are active, a constant stream of chemicals and hormones rush around inside the body and brain to keep us alert, ready to react and stay safe. When we are no longer in real-time danger, we need to recognize that is the case and actively change our inner processing—mind, body and emotions. Our goal is to unlock the neurological loop taking us back to fear and danger, which is harmful to our health. The key to being in charge of our well-being is to be aware of ourselves and our reactions and break the stress response.

After a traumatic event, we may feel fear on many levels. Until we recognize and move through it, we can carry that fear and trauma with us from childhood to old age.

Fear showing up as panic attacks or being afraid to get into a vehicle after being rear-ended, as happened with one client, is understandable and can quickly be resolved. A child whose father died in an accident when she was four years old carried the trauma as fear of being abandoned, of something happening to her mother and of feeling unsafe in the world. The matter was finally addressed when she was seventeen years old.

Driving after my car accident required planning and practice. I drove at a snail's pace to begin with and chose the best weather and road conditions. After applying some of the strategies outlined in this book, one day, to my surprise, I found that I felt safe again and was perfectly happy behind the wheel.

Other people's fear can be contagious, whether due to their own trauma or because they are concerned for our well-being. If we feel fear it is important to recognize its origin, to own it and then work through it. Not so that we can be reckless in the future but so that we can be responsible, empowered and trauma-free.

We don't have to personally experience horrific events to be traumatized. We see this in many children and teachers in schools in the United States who have lock-down practices, are searched for guns, and read about and see images of kids being shot and killed by other kids with guns. Many of them walk in fear every day.

EXERCISE: MOVING THROUGH FEAR

We have to feel comfortable, relaxed and safe to be able to release fear. The three steps in chapter 2—breathing, deep relaxation and creating a safe place—are the first steps towards moving through fear.

In a state of ease, observe your thoughts and feelings as they flow through you, identify the fearful ones and ask yourself the following questions:

- Is this fear real in this moment? (Usually the answer is no.)
- Is this fear related to a past event or old belief? (Usually the answer is yes.)
- What have I learnt and what can I do differently now to feel fearless and safe? (Think of three things that will eradicate the fear. Imagine doing them and feeling fearless and safe. Sometimes the answers are really simple, such as keeping the lights on or having the phone by your bed.)
- In your mind, do those things differently many times, feeling fearless and safe, to break the neurological trauma fear loop.

Desensitizing Traumatic Memories and Reactions

The impact on the senses, mind, body and emotions from a traumatic event can be powerful. Past, present and future are diminished to insignificance by the enormity of the trauma.

When we can bring ourselves into the present moment and have the ability to feel relaxed, calm and safe, we begin to have control over our response to shock and trauma. Physical pain—whether from childbirth, an accident, surgery or other event—tends to naturally fade from memory over time, as does emotional pain. But if the pain or trauma hangs around week after week, remains vivid and causes reactions, we need to take action.

EXERCISE: HEALING OLD MEMORIES

Here is an exercise to heal old memories that I guide people through and use myself. Before you start, sit and become comfortable. Then follow the steps for breathing and deep relaxation in chapter 2. You will start by choosing two memories, then continue on with the exercise.

Memory 1: Remember a time you felt comfortable, safe and happy. Where were you? How old were you? What could you see? What did you feel? Were there any sounds you heard? If you can see the memory, imagine drifting into it as in a dream. Step into it and be there now. See, feel, hear and move in that place and memory. Begin to make the memory powerful and strong and feel really good. Notice how and where in yourself you feel good. Do you feel it in your heart, your mind, your body or your stomach (quite likely all of them)? Remember these feelings.

Memory 2: Think of a time closer to the present when you felt fabulous. Where were you? How old were you? What could you see? What did you feel? Were there any sounds you heard? If you can see the memory, imagine drifting into it as in a dream, and be there now. See, feel, hear and move in that place and memory. Begin to make that memory powerful and strong and feel really good. Notice how and where in yourself you feel good. Is it in your heart, your mind, your body or your stomach (quite likely all of them)? Remember these feelings.

Take your mind to these memories often, and make them potent, powerful and strong as you feel amazingly good in the remembering. Only once this step is easy for you and you can access the memories and positive feelings whenever you choose, are you ready to use your mind to diminish the power of the trauma.

Note that this exercise is not for the time immediately after trauma; allow the natural healing process to work first. If traumatic memories still flash into your mind three or four weeks after, this exercise may be helpful at that time.

Before you begin, decide which positive memory you want to step into first to feel positive and strong. Next, decide whether you want to imagine yourself high above, like an eagle, looking down at a miniscule version of the traumatic event way below, or to imagine a tiny version on a movie screen. From whichever vantage point you choose, the image you see will be very, very small, like ants on the ground or crawling across a screen. The image will be black and white with no sound. When you run the scene, you will make it go super-fast backwards and forwards, backwards and forwards. Tiny images, no feelings.

The Desensitizing Process

Start with the powerful, positive, strong memory from the steps above. Imagine it until you feel great.

Quickly, in seconds, from a safe, comfortable and distant vantage point, run through the negative or traumatic scenario, viewing it from high above or on a tiny screen, with no sound, no feeling, and running the image super-fast backwards and forwards. You are in control. You can stop any time you choose and step back into the wonderful memory where you feel really strong, safe and good. Make sure you always end the process experiencing a powerful, positive, strong memory—and feeling great.

Run through the process once or twice, and follow up daily for three or seven days. Always start with positive, powerful and wonderful feelings, then imagine a quick, tiny, black-and-white view of the trauma with no sounds, sensations or feelings, and end with positive, powerful and wonderful feelings.

If you have problems with this process, don't struggle with it. I recommend you find a hypnotherapist to guide you through one of a number of desensitizing exercises. Ideally, get recommendations, always check the credentials of the practitioner, and be sure you feel comfortable working with whomever you choose.

Handling Stress and Building Resilience

As I mentioned previously, experiencing trauma normally activates the stress response because of the shock and fear factors. Once you have handled the immediate shock and fear of an event, the recovery process deals with the aftershock, which includes both the memory of the event and continuing stress reactions. Self-awareness and stress resilience are lasting lifetime gifts once we have moved through trauma.

Now let's review my understanding of stress, trauma and post-traumatic stress disorder:

- **Stress** is the result of imbalance between the mind, body, emotions and spirit. Stress can slowly accumulate, causing pressure and symptoms resulting directly or indirectly from the stress response.
- **Trauma** is the result of an impactful, perhaps horrifying, event that causes shock, fear and feelings of loss of control and helplessness, all of which activate the stress response.
- **Post-Traumatic Stress Disorder** arises from one or more traumatic events that deeply impact the neurological, physiological and emotional state of being, causing spontaneous flashbacks and mental, emotional and physical reactions to triggers such as sights, sounds, smells, tastes and feelings.

THE STRESS WISDOM MODEL

Whatever the category of stress, we are affected holistically. In other words, whether we are stressed out from trying to meet an unrealistic deadline for a project, have lost our job because our employer has declared bankruptcy, or a parent has just died from a heart attack, we are likely to be impacted mentally, physically, emotionally and spiritually. For example, in the case of trying to meet an unrealistic deadline, we may not be able to think clearly and we may begin to hyperventilate. Our blood pressure may rise, and we may feel angry, tearful or panicked.

It is virtually impossible to address a specific problem when we are hyper-vigilant, anxious, running on adrenalin or under the influence of the stress response. However, once we are able to be calm and relaxed on demand and feel safe, we can more easily handle issues that need to be resolved or healed. If we suddenly feel anxious, we know that we can change those feelings and quickly feel calm again.

The Mind

The previous section discussed fear and safety, but there are many reactions to stress. Some of the mental symptoms of trauma and stress are discussed below and include suggestions for handling them.

ANXIETY, HEADACHES, AND MIGRAINES

To relieve anxiety, headaches and migraines due to mental or emotional overload or overwhelm, we need to still the mind. When the mind slows down, it can become calm and regain clarity, which can also help to increase focus, improve concentration and ease memory problems.

Water can be wonderfully healing for headaches and migraines. My favourite way to ease a migraine is to soak in a warm bath, with the back of my head in the water. I find that I naturally begin to relax physically and mentally as I listen to the sound of water running from the tap and focus my attention on the feeling of the warm water on my skin and head. My mind is distracted from worry or pressure in the present moment, and my thoughts slow down as my head, hands, feet and body reach a common, comfortable temperature.

Standing under a shower of warm water is not as relaxing to me as soaking in a bath, but it is a good way to focus the mind on feeling the pressure and temperature of the water and achieve a common temperature for head, hands, feet and body (which negates the stress response of cold hands and feet).

Sleeping after a bath or shower can be the final step to releasing tension. As we sleep, the mind re-organizes and relaxes, and we can wake up refreshed.

Here are some simple tips to relieve headaches and migraines:

- Apply lavender and peppermint oils to the back of the neck, wrists and forehead.
- Do alternate nostril breathing.
- Drink caffeine or hot water with a sprinkling of chili powder.
- Drink ginger tea with lemon juice to help settle the stomach.
- Apply ice packs at the back of the neck and forehead to soothe.
- Put your head under the cold tap for a few moments to lower its temperature.

For many people, soaking in warm water proves to be the most deeply relaxing and healing way to ease migraines and headaches following trauma. As with so many things, this is a matter of personal preference and finding what works best for you.

Affirmation: I am becoming calm.

INABILITY TO FOCUS, POOR CONCENTRATION AND POOR MEMORY

Symptoms of stress and trauma include the inability to focus and poor long- or short-term memory. It can be scary to find that we can't remember something that happened a couple of days ago or what someone said moments beforehand. It is unnerving to be unable to concentrate, to read more than a couple of sentences without losing track or to phase out of conversations, the radio or television programs.

One way to handle these symptoms is to simply breathe, relax and know that these are normal, passing, stress-related symptoms.

Affirmation: This will pass.

BECOMING A WORKAHOLIC

In times of stress, some people focus on work and develop workaholic behavior. For a while this can distract from the memories, thoughts and feelings related to trauma. But in the end it creates an unbalanced life and considerably increases overall stress levels. Simply understanding that too much focus on work is a stress reaction that you may have fallen into can bring understanding, awareness and change.

The exercises in this book, including breathing, relaxing and the walking exercise later in this section can help return you to balance.

Affirmation: It is safe to be balanced.

BEING OVERLY LOGICAL

Shock and extreme stress can lock the brain into left-brain functioning, where logical thinking occurs (see appendix 4). Normally, the left (logical) and right (emotional/creative) sides of the brain interrelate on an ongoing basis. One way to release a lock in the left brain can be to walk while swinging your arms, with the opposite hand and knee more or less touching (left knee/right hand, right knee/left hand). You can do this walking on the spot, too. Two to five minutes of this exercise is often enough to shift the brain back to a fluid left/right connection. (Note: This exercise is helpful for shifting mental and emotional stuck states.)

Affirmation: It is safe to feel.

APATHY, LACK OF ENERGY

Stress and trauma can make the most basic things overwhelming, such as washing, dressing, cooking, eating and performing the smallest tasks. There is nothing wrong with you; these are normal responses to trauma and high stress. You have had a shock, and your whole being is reacting. Be gentle with yourself. Accept help. Just do what you can. Sleep, breathe, relax, cry or get really angry (anger is energizing).

Affirmation: This will pass.

FEELING DEPRESSED, PROCRASTINATING, GIVING UP

During a traumatic event and immediately afterwards, we seldom have time or want to bother to care for ourselves or to eat and sleep properly. Adrenalin is keeping us going. It is absolutely natural to have an energy slump following such an energetic push while running on empty. We are being reminded to take care of ourselves now, to get enough sleep and rest, eat well, drink water and take gentle exercise. However, if, after a short period of nourish and nurture, you feel seriously depressed, please consult with your healthcare professional.

Affirmation: I take small, consistent steps to care for myself.

REVISITING THE TRAUMATIC EVENT

One reaction to trauma is revisiting and replaying the traumatic or stressful event in our minds. There is a fine line between replaying a traumatic experience in our mind as we release it and obsessing about it. The difference between one and the other is significant and plays a vital role in whether we become swallowed up by stress and trauma or free ourselves from what has happened and move on in a healthy way. The key is mental discipline.

When we think of an experience, whether real or imagined, our brain and body respond. If we imagine relaxing on a beach, our whole being will begin to feel relaxed. If we think about a threatening event, we feel fear, and instantly and automatically, the stress response is activated.

For this reason, it is crucial that we are disciplined in how we think. How often we allow ourselves to revisit a trauma in our minds is directly related to how often we retraumatize ourselves and how tense, anxious and stressed we feel.

Like particles of dust floating in a sunbeam, thoughts are always moving through our minds. But unlike particles of dust, our thoughts often follow set tracks. We may smell food cooking, think of supper, and decide to buy wine. Then we remember the last time we had a glass wine with a particular friend we had an argument with and haven't spoken to since—and we feel depressed and misunderstood and regret what we said. The next time we have a glass of wine, our thoughts may follow exactly the same track slowly, or we may immediately feel depressed, misunderstood and regretful.

For this reason, making a decision to be aware of our thoughts and choosing not to re-traumatize ourselves unnecessarily can be helpful. If we need to release or resolve a particular issue, we can set aside regular time each day to do so. Ideally, do this while sitting in the same chair or standing in the same place. This creates a sensory/neurological connection to ease the process. Then, if the related feeling or thought pops up, we can remind ourselves that we will be dealing with that later, say "shift" and send our thoughts to something we love—a sunset, a kitten, a child, a piece of music—and consciously get into the loving experience by seeing, hearing, feeling, touching, tasting, smelling and imagining being there.

This discipline can seem extraordinarily challenging to begin with. We are breaking a lifetime habit. All too often we cling to a problem, going around in mental circles trying to resolve it. But we can't resolve a problem with the same mindset that sees or created the problem. The truth is, letting go provides space for the tangle of the issue in the mind to unravel, and it gives us moments of peace. How often has the answer to a problem come when you were relaxing on the beach, walking through the woods or soaking in the bath?

When we are recovering from trauma, thoughts of the trauma, or grief or loss, may keep coming to mind. We can gently acknowledge them. Sometimes we will be able to shift our thinking and sometimes not. That is fine. The recovery process is a flexible and gradual one.

Affirmation: I gradually release trauma from my mind.

Following is a tip for dealing with nightmares or frightening thoughts in a fun way. I most often share this game with children, but adults can play, too.

If you have a frightening memory or nightmare, choose to change it while having fun in the process. If a person in your mind or dreams looks frightening, be creative and play with the image. Give the person green hair, purple ears, a hat with a huge daisy hanging over their nose and enormous orange clown shoes. Keep on adding to and changing the image until it makes you laugh or just seems silly. If they have a frightening voice, make them whisper, sing or croak like a frog. If they are chasing you, turn around and see them the size of a tiny ball, and sit them on a tree stump.

You can also draw the images and write words such as "I am safe" and "I am strong".

Affirmation: I can change my mind.

The Body

The physical aspects of the stress response are now considered to be the root cause of most illnesses. There are numerous changes that occur within the body when the fight, flight or freeze response kicks in, which it does every time real or imagined danger is felt (see appendix 1).

Under stress, changes occur in our breathing, circulation, senses, heart, organs, digestive system, hormone production, skin, muscles and skeletal structure. Sometimes these changes can be frightening. Sometimes they can even be life-threatening, such as a rise in blood pressure.

Below are some of the physical responses that can occur when we are stressed or traumatized. It is helpful to recognize what happens within our own bodies at such times. Often we get early warning signs.

DIGESTION

Immediately following severe stress or trauma, we are frequently unable to hold down food or liquid, and this can be frightening. Simply knowing that it is a natural process and only a temporary phase can ease anxiety. We may also have diarrhea or need to empty our bladder frequently. Stomach cramps, bloating or constipation may occur if we haven't eaten for a few days. The theory is that by not digesting food in times of extreme danger, we reserve our energy to be able to run or fight.

Here are some tips to aid your digestion:

- Follow the breathing and relaxation steps in chapter 2 to relax the body and release stress.
- Drink water, hot or cold, with lemon juice or ginger added if you like.
- Add electrolytes to a glass of water if you still are not able to eat after a couple of days.
- Drink broth, vegetable and fruit juices, and soups.
- Avoid caffeine, alcohol and sugar (caffeine and sugar alter chemical components within the brain and body; alcohol is a depressant).
- Eat small, light, nutritious meals.
- Get advice from a healthcare professional, nutritionist or dietician on the value of taking vitamin B for the nervous system, multivitamin and mineral supplements to boost the immune system and prebiotics and probiotics to keep your gut healthy.
- If you have constipation, walking for five to fifteen minutes a couple of times a day may

be helpful. Also be sure to drink plenty of water and consume fruit and vegetables in the form of juices, raw or lightly cooked.

Affirmation: I relax and digest with ease.

CIRCULATION

When shock hits, blood leaves the extremities and goes straight to the muscles and heart. This is what makes our feet and hands feel cold and can often lead to feeling cold in general. To help keep yourself warm, wear extra clothes and socks, wrap up in a blanket, or soak your hands in warm water.

Affirmation: I take care of myself and keep warm.

BREATHING AND TENSION

When we are afraid, we tend to breathe shallowly or hold our breath and become physically tense. The first time I drove after my car accident, I was incredibly anxious and tense. I had to pull off the road every four or five minutes because I felt so uncomfortable. My shoulders were up by my ears, my hands were gripping the steering wheel tightly, and I was breathing very fast and shallowly. I had to consciously unclench my hands, lower my shoulders, breathe slowly and deeply, relax and tell myself, "I am safe". Off I would drive, only to have to stop again a few minutes later!

Here are some tips to help with your breathing:

- Notice your breathing. Is it fast and shallow or deep, low and following a gentle rhythm? If your breathing is fast, high and shallow, consciously spend a few moments to change the way you are breathing to deep, low and slow.
- Be aware of your body. How tense is it? Where are you holding tension? Then breathe, relax and imagine that you are breathing warmth, relaxation and comfort into any areas that are tense.
- Physical tension can be eased with Reiki, massage or by soaking in a float tank.

Affirmation: I release tension as I relax my muscles and breathe gently and deeply.

PHYSICAL PAIN

When we have physical pain in our bodies, we tend to tense our muscles and hold ourselves in an unbalanced way, as if to protect whatever is uncomfortable.

Deep relaxation allows the muscles to relax as we release tension. At the same time, our bodies can realign. After I have run a group relaxation session or given an individual session, people frequently tell me that their pain has gone entirely or has significantly decreased, whether they're lying on the floor or sitting on a chair.

Here are some tips to help you to deeply relax:

- Sit or lie down comfortably and take yourself through a deep relaxation. Either follow the steps for deep relaxation in chapter 2 or listen to a recording, your own or someone else's. Imagine each muscle relaxing, pain diminishing and dissolving and feeling more comfortable and at ease.
- Have a Reiki session or a gentle massage. This will help to relax all of your muscles and take your attention away from the pain. A client who was an amputee found massage to be the most impactful step he took towards healing and regaining strength throughout his body.
- Soak in a float tank. This is a great way to ease pain.
- Laugh! Laughter releases feel-good,

pain-killing chemicals called endorphins. A client who had injured his back and was waiting for surgery found that laughter was the most effective pain killer. Those endorphins are powerful! Norman Cousins, an American author, booked into a hotel to watch comedy while he waited to die—except, contrary to his doctor's diagnosis and expectation, he didn't die. He fully recovered and went on to study the benefits of laughter.

Affirmation: I relax, remember to laugh and gently release pain.

THE SENSES

The stress response heightens our senses: sight, hearing, smell, taste and touch. This can explain how, when we are shocked and afraid, we can hear a pin or leaf drop, while we wouldn't normally be able to do so, however hard we tried.

After we have been living on high alert for a while, the senses dull and we may find that we can't taste food or smell the roses in the garden, and maybe we can't see as clearly as we normally do. These changes can happen gradually. On one occasion, I realized I needed to deal with stress when I was changing the kitty litter and couldn't smell anything.

Here are some tips to help you support your sensory system:

- Do a sensory check every now and again. How well can you smell, taste, hear, feel and see?
- If you notice a significant dulling of one or more of your senses, practice the breathing and deep relaxation steps in chapter 2.
- Be sure to get enough sleep.
- Ask yourself if you are eating well and drinking water. If you are not, make a conscious effort to do so.
- Check whether anything is bothering you. If so, decide on three actions to take that will address the problem.

As mentioned previously, the heightening and then dulling of the senses is a normal response to trauma, but we need to get out of that stress response so that we can begin to heal.

Affirmation: All my senses function optimally.

WALKING

If you are not injured or recovering from surgery, walking at whatever pace is easy and comfortable can be wonderfully beneficial. The movement assists breathing, circulation and the overall functioning of the heart, digestion, organs, muscles and body.

Studies have found that if we spend time imagining that we are exercising, our bodies will show significant improvement in fitness, not far short of the benefit gained from having actually exercised. This is wonderful, because it means that people who have been injured or had surgery can use their minds to follow an exercise regimen, and their muscles will actually benefit from doing so.

Here are some tips for getting benefits from walking:

- Set time aside to walk regularly. If you don't normally do any exercise or have had surgery, begin your new routine gently, and gradually increase the time and incline you walk.
- Before you begin imagining an exercise practice, it is necessary to be in a comfortable and relaxed state.
- Mentally think of the exercise you want to follow, then imagine yourself doing it.

Imagine each move and how your body feels, what you see, maybe what you hear. Imagine seeing and feeling the specific muscles moving and getting stronger. Imagine or feel your breath and heartbeat. You can choose where you want to walk: around the block, on a beach in Bali or along a mountain trail.

Affirmation: I enjoy exercise and feel the benefits.

The Emotions

Following trauma and during recovery, we may feel as though we are on an emotional rollercoaster. Our sense of inner balance and calm may vanish for short or long periods of time, and when we find ourselves reacting in totally unfamiliar ways, we may feel afraid. For example, a person who is accustomed to running the home, handling a job, caring for kids and connecting with friends and family with ease may find it scary when they burst into tears because the traffic light turned red as they were about to drive across a junction, or when someone knocked into them as they were walking out of the grocery store.

This heightened sensitivity is all part of the stress response following shock, trauma or stress. It is a sign that recovery and healing have yet to be reached. As we return to balance, we may feel dull or numb. Worry not—all these feelings are normal and natural following a traumatic event.

Whatever issues we are dealing with, we need to accept that our feelings are constantly changing. As we rebalance, our feelings will become less extreme. In the meantime, it is a matter of riding the wave, accepting and understanding what is going on, nourishing and nurturing ourselves on all levels and taking easy steps to help ourselves heal.

Know and expect that it is possible to heal and be happy again. The following are some thoughts and actions to consider.

ANGER AND RAGE

Anger is commonly seen as a level above sadness. Whereas sadness saps our energy and even our will to live, anger gives us energy. We could also look on anger and rage as raw stress reactions—the "fight" in fight-or-flight. We may be surprised when someone begins to rant and rage about a trivial matter, but when we learn that they recently lost a child, it becomes easy to understand that they are getting by as best they can. Following trauma, we need to release the anger held in our bodies.

Below are three exercises for releasing anger and rage. Don't be surprised if your anger turns into other feelings whilst doing any of the following exercises, or if a variety of images, scenes and words come to you. (Note: Please check with your medical advisor before doing the physical exercise if you have heart problems or high blood pressure.)

1. Choose one of the following: beat a pillow with a bat or a fist; scream while inside a car, at an isolated place or into a pillow; chop wood; box a punch bag; run; bike. Pick one or more of these choices, and really put effort into the task for five to twenty minutes, depending on which one you choose. Afterwards, you will likely feel spent and relaxed. Have a drink of water, breathe and deeply relax (as in chapter 2) for five to twenty minutes.
2. Write in detail about what you feel angry about and how the anger feels. When complete, shred or burn the paper.
3. Draw or paint the feelings of anger and the related trauma story, then do a drawing or painting of feelings of love. Compare the

> two and notice the differences in colours, shapes and, above all, your feelings as you look at them. When complete, shred or burn the picture depicting your feelings of anger.

It is helpful to do these exercises in the same place and at the same time each day, whether or not you feel angry—the anger will come up. Gradually reduce the time for the exercise over a number of days; don't stop suddenly.

Affirmation: As I release anger I feel loving and calm.

RESENTMENT AND HATRED

The feelings of resentment and hatred are the opposite of love. When a small child has been hurt by a sibling, they may lash out, say they hate them and carry a resentful story around for a while. They feel unloved by the one who hurt them.

A person who has been shocked by a traumatic event may well feel unloved and will need to accept that bad things can happen to good people. They will need to come to terms with the fact that it was unlucky that they were in that place at the time of the impersonal trauma.

Normally, as you heal from trauma, resentment and hatred dissolve. However, if they linger too long, there are things you can do to help them shift.

Here are some tips for dealing with resentment and hatred:

- Give yourself permission to hate for a little while longer. Do the entire anger exercise of beating, boxing or chopping for five to twenty minutes every day. There is a strong possibility that the subject of your hatred will be the one you find yourself beating up. That is fine. Allow the feelings to work out of your body.
- Imagine the person you hate or resent as a little child. Think of a game you loved playing as a child, and imagine the two of you playing that game together: two little kids, laughing, being distracted by fun stuff and enjoying being together.

Affirmation: As I heal, I become filled with love.

SADNESS, GRIEF AND LOSS

Very often sadness comes in waves and can be triggered by our thoughts or senses. A piece of music playing on the radio may bring tears, cause us to want to sleep away the wave of pain, or to numb it out in some other way. The loss of a loved one leaves an emptiness that will be filled by love and memories recalled over time after the intensity of the loss has slightly diminished. There is truth in the words "time heals". But when we are immersed in the intensity of grief, they seem meaningless and provide cold comfort.

One of the most chilling things to occur after loss of a loved one is that people may avoid you or ignore your loss altogether. This seems to negate the person you are mourning and render you less of who you were at the very time you are trying to keep your feet on the ground and cope alone.

Here are some tips to help keep your love alive and move through your sadness, grief and loss:

- ✧ Have a photograph and a memento of this special person. Place the photo beside your bed or on a small table. Carry the memento with you everywhere—on a necklace or in a pocket or purse. This helps you to feel in touch with them.
- ✧ Have conversations with them in your head or in a journal (or both), and tell them about your day, the little things and big things,

how much you love them, how you miss them. Allow tears to flow freely. Be real. Be angry they have left you, and tell them so if that is how you feel. Then, share with them how much special moments spent together meant to you—things they said, little things they did, their funny sayings and habits. If there is something you meant to tell them, this is the time to do so. This can become a routine. Spend as much or as little time every day as you want. By following this practice, you keep the person in your heart and your life, and then it doesn't matter if other people fail to see you or talk about your loss. Remember to touch the memento as you think of them.

- Form a habit, or else act spontaneously, and visit places you went to together, perhaps a beach or sitting on a bench watching the sunset. To begin with, tears may flow, but they will be tears of love and loss as you re-experience shared memories. This can be healing. It will also ensure that you don't lock the pain in your heart, build a barrier of avoidance and cause future health problems.

Affirmation: Love lasts.

PAST UNRESOLVED EMOTIONAL ISSUES OR TRAUMAS

During the recovery process from trauma, you may become aware of old, unresolved issues. Very often there is something linking the past and present, such as circumstances, a person or emotions that are similar or even the same.

Often once they are in your awareness, and after dealing with the most recent trauma, past issues naturally dissolve or can be quickly resolved using new-found skills.

Here are some tips to help you deal with past issues:

- Make a brief note of the past issue that came to mind. You can look at it later, when you are feeling calm and balanced. Then, ask yourself whether there is anything you can do in the present time to resolve or heal the issue, or whether you can let it go. If so, take the action, or imagine letting go - a kite flying in the breeze, a balloon floating away, or a rock being dropped into a stream. If the time doesn't feel right to let go, keep the note of the issue, refer to it later and see if you are ready to let go then.

- If you find that the memory is disturbing to you, consider whether any of the life skills you now have, that you didn't have at the time, will be helpful in releasing it. If so, try them out in your mind.
- Alternatively, to release the past trauma, seek appropriate professional help.

Affirmation: As I become calm and balanced, old issues dissolve and have no power over me.

GUILT

When we have survived tragedy and horror and others have not been so lucky, it is natural to feel guilty for being alive. Similarly, if others have been injured and we have not been, we may feel guilty. After the shock comes recognition of what has happened, and sometimes the guilt, that has to be processed and released over time, arises later.

Generally, there is no apparent reason for the hand of fate and why one person survives and another does not. No one person is better than another or deserves a grander outcome or a longer life.

Whatever our religious and spiritual beliefs, it may be helpful to recognize that now that we have been spared, we can choose to be the very best we can be. This does not mean to become mega-rich or famous. It means to become kind, compassionate and loving, to see the best and be forgiving, and to live as a vulnerable, honest human being.

Here are some tips for dealing with guilt:

- Instead of holding onto guilt, think about what you will choose as your path and purpose to live by from now on.
- If you feel you wronged or treated someone unkindly and you want to apologize, even though it may not be advisable or possible to speak with them in person, you could light a candle or write what you would like to say to them and read it silently or out loud.

Dr. Hew Len, an American psychologist, followed the Ho'oponopono practice of repentance, forgiveness, gratitude and love by saying the following as a prayer and form of distance healing: "I am sorry, please forgive me, thank you, I love you".

Affirmation: I am in the right place at the right time, and I always do my best.

EMOTIONAL FLEEING

Despair, apathy, feeling helpless, going emotionally numb—all of these feelings can be grouped in the stress response category of "flee". There is no physical running away, but there is a profound sense of giving up or fleeing from the present reality.

These feelings are natural and normal as responses to shock, trauma and stress, but they are "stuck" states. We need to move through them as gently and quickly as possible and into a more empowering phase of healing.

Beginning to take action to care for yourself and moving towards healing can feel as though you are moving mountains, but I urge you to make the effort—moment by moment, day by day. If you stop, put in extra effort to start again. Stop and praise yourself after each successful step. Feel good.

Here are some tips for general self-care:

- Regularly practice the steps in chapter 2: breathing, deep relaxation and feeling safe. After every practice, stop, breathe and praise yourself for completing this.
- Drink water and eat healthy snacks and meals.

- Avoid alcohol and sugar. Alcohol is a depressant and sugar alters mood and body chemistry.
- Make sure you get enough sleep. If necessary, ask your healthcare professional for sleeping pills.
- Have an aromatherapy massage; light candles; bring flowers into your home.
- Decide what is important and easy to achieve today. Start with just one thing. Write it down. When will you do it? Write that down, then do it. Celebrate when you are done! (Note: When we are in shock or trauma, it is unhelpful to expect great things to be achieved before we have recovered. Chunk down everything into small pieces and be super-happy with every small achievement. Make sure every task you set yourself is easy and enjoyable.)

Affirmation: My energy is returning moment by moment.

The Spirit

My sense of spirit is of an intangible, ever-present part of me that can be touched and felt in unexpected moments.

We had just reached a viewpoint in Banff Provincial Park in Canada. A breathtaking 360-degree view of snowcapped mountains surrounded us. Tears spontaneously spilled down my cheeks. My spirit was deeply touched. That feeling cannot be reproduced through movies or photographs, although it can be remembered when I am still and peaceful.

Our spirit affects our energy, will to live and ability to unexpectedly recover from an illness. A lady in her nineties had been given three weeks to live. However, shortly after her diagnosis, she discovered that her granddaughter was expecting a baby girl, who was going to be named after her great-grandma. This lady was so excited by the news that her energy and vitality returned, and she outlived all expectations.

Our spirit is expressed through joy, a sense of awe, creativity, spontaneity, inner energy and enthusiasm. When we drag ourselves through life one dreary, exhausting day after another, we are most definitely disconnected from our spirit.

Many things can gradually drain our spirit: abandonment, diminishing relationships or financial pressures, for example. The shock and horror of trauma tends to instantly block access to our spirit. Then, as we tread the path to recovery through nurturing the mind, body and emotions, we begin to rekindle our spirit one tiny flicker at a time.

Don't worry if you are unable to access your sense of awe and '*aha*' for a while. You can listen to beautiful music, be immersed in the wonders of nature and remain stony and untouched. Then one evening, whilst sitting on a bench overlooking the ocean, you may feel the sense of beauty and wonder being absorbed and felt through your whole being. Your spirit has returned!

Here are some tips to call your spirit back:

- Play with little children or pets, splash in puddles or rediscover one of your favorite childhood games.
- Spend time in nature. Be aware of the sights, sounds, smells and feelings. If you are in the city, look up at the sky and notice the clouds, birds and colors and feel the temperature of the air on your skin, or look down and see the plants growing through cracks on the sidewalk or a wall. Begin to become aware of beauty.
- Meditate. There are many ways to meditate, but one is to sit comfortably, be still and gently breathe. Observe your thoughts passing through your mind. This is an effective way to still mental chatter.
- Yoga helps you to focus inwardly on your body and your breathing.

- Find something creative to be absorbed in: draw, paint, cook, create a mandala, sing or play music.

Affirmation: My spirit feels wonder and awe and is the spark of life.

Summary

This chapter includes the essential steps towards recovery from trauma, helping you to develop lifetime skills to recognize stress and build stress resilience. You can learn to move easily and lightly from mind to body, to emotions, to spirit and back again.

Remember to always choose the strategies and tips that seem easy, simple and enjoyable. Try things that you think may not apply to you. In doing so, you will reinforce existing strengths as you build new ones. Never struggle. Be gentle and patient with yourself.

CHAPTER 4

Stage 3: Change, Wisdom and Peace

Trauma powerfully impacts the mind, body, emotions and spirit, so the healing process normally takes considerably longer than it would to, say, heal a broken bone. It is necessary to heal the neurological damage, ease physical and emotional pain and to call our spirit back.

During the healing process we often lurch forward with one success only to find ourselves circling back to something that we have already worked on, something that is less painful than before but still requires attention. This is why it is so important to celebrate every small achievement along the way, even to the point of keeping a record in a journal that we can look back on when we're feeling discouraged.

For example, if we have used every ounce of courage and energy to cope with the death of a spouse, we may find ourselves feeling numb immediately afterwards, retreating to sitting and staring into space. This is the time to accept our feelings and nourish and nurture ourselves with loving kindness in the best way we can. Even though we may feel depressed or low, we can write in our journal small steps or achievements such as "I never thought I would be able to ________, but I did!" By doing this, we show ourselves that we have strength, stamina and courage.

Life will never be exactly the same after trauma has exploded into our lives. Everything may have changed almost beyond recognition, but by far the greatest transformation will be invisible and within us and will happen gradually over time.

It is almost as though the Divine gives in the same ratio as it takes; the deeper the wound, the greater the gift. From the almost unbearable pain of losing both of his children, one man found peace by creating exquisite sculptures. This helped him through his darkest moments and later became his passion and livelihood.

The mere fact that we have plunged to the depths and somehow struggled through fear and pain, risen to the surface and stayed afloat, builds trust in our resilience.

Trauma leads us into the dark night of the soul as we look death in the eye. After a lifetime of being afraid of dying, many people accept their mortality and this opens exploration into religion and spirituality and possibly establishes new beliefs.

One of the most consistent changes that I have found in trauma survivors and thrivers is that they reassess their priorities and values. Things that had seemed important become trivial. Recently someone said that, since her sudden illness, only two things matter to her: her health and her family. This was from a lady who was constantly multitasking and juggling family, two jobs, a rigid fitness regimen and a couple of hobbies. After her traumatic diagnosis she rebuilt her life with new values, developed new strengths and created a gentler and more loving way to treat herself. This can be one of the gifts of trauma.

When we have grasped and live by new values, we often look back at our old way of life with wonder. We need to forgive ourselves for our behaviors in the past, when we were in a different phase of life. We always do our very best.

Once we have moved through the stages of recovery we are likely to be kinder and more compassionate with everyone, not just family and friends. We begin to recognize that the person who is rude to us may be dealing with their own pain. We accept that hurt people hurt people. We want to help create a gentler and kinder planet for all. We can imagine walking in another's moccasins. This is stepping into wisdom.

Mind, Body, Emotions and Spirit (MBES)

My car accident affected me physically, mentally, emotionally and spiritually. The pain was such that the smallest amount of physical movement was uncomfortable. Mentally, I was happy to read or watch small amounts of light, humorous material but War and Peace or anything requiring concentration or calculation would have been beyond my scope. Emotionally I felt vulnerable. Energy, creativity and joy (under my spirit category) were mostly absent. I was in survival and recovery mode.

Appendix 3 shows the interconnectedness between mind, body, emotions and spirit. I have found that very often the lives of my stressed-out clients are out of balance primarily in one area. A meditation teacher, high on spirituality (S) and financial skills (M), but who's emotional life (E) was a chaotic mess. A medical doctor had the work, money (M) and love (E), but over-extended himself to the point that he was barely conscious of his body (B) (which was eighty pounds overweight). An executive with a well-paid job (M), felt highly pressured. He found laying people off work was a painful process and, combined with his lack of self-care, it was not surprising to me when he had a heart attack.

Lack of balance has been a common thread connecting most of my clients. I have found that seeking to maintain flexible, comfortable balance on an ongoing basis has been a key to their recovery. Very often the greatest success has come when people focus away from their stress for a while. This allows them to focus on other areas of their life and return to the problem once they are generally stronger and feeling more resilient. Then, what felt like a mountain seems to have shrunk to nothing more than a manageable and silly glitch.

This section provides a number of simple, speedy check-ins to assess your stress and level of balance. When you understand your stress, you are in a position to build resilience. There is guidance to follow to make the process as comfortable and easy as possible. I suggest you bring the practice into your daily life. Think of it in the same way you would a rocket heading to the moon. Adjustments are constant to stay in balance.

Check In and Rebalance

To retain or attain a peaceful state, it is essential to be self-aware—not narcissistically so, but for overall well-being. Regularly checking in with oneself is the best way that I know of doing this. Depending on what's going on in your life, you may choose to check in once a day or on the hour, every hour, until you become calm and balanced.

Here are some simple tips for checking in:

Sit comfortably and breathe deeply, rhythmically and gently. Develop a scale in your mind, an inner reference of 0 (bad) to 10 (excellent).

Ask yourself the following questions, and answer on a scale of 0 (bad) to 10 (excellent). Research has shown that spontaneous answers are most accurate so be sure to answer the questions quickly.

- How do I feel overall? ________________
- How do I feel mentally? ______________
- How do I feel physically? _____________
- How do I feel emotionally? ___________
- How do I feel spiritually? _____________

Look at the numbers you have written down. For any answer below 6, refer back to the relevant part of the stress section in chapter 3. Reread it, sift through the tips and strategies and choose something easy and enjoyable that you can do to increase your sense of well-being.

Aim to feel 6 or above on the scale for all sections (MBES). Maybe you will just need to think of something you love or to breathe deeply. Over time, you will develop your own inner tool kit to feel good fast.

Inflammation

We can apply the scale of 0 (low inflammation) to 10 (highly inflamed) to questions about inflammation. This is related to how agitated we feel; suppressed feelings of anger, blame or resentment; and physical aches and pains.

Sit comfortably and breathe deeply, rhythmically and gently. Ask yourself the following questions, again answering them quickly and honestly.

- How inflamed do I feel in general?

  ____

- How inflamed are my thoughts and words?

  ____

- How inflamed does my body feel?

  ____

- How inflamed are my emotions?

  ____

- How suppressed is my spirit?

  ____

Aim to get and keep your inflammation low on the scale, around or below 2 or 3. If your answers are above 4, refer to the appropriate section in chapter 3 to find suggestions and tips to bring a sense of cool and calm to your being.

Inflammation, whether in our thinking, body or emotions, is harmful. Anger is useful only to right a wrong, fight off intruders and similar purposes. An inflamed body and inflamed emotions can harm our health and need to be soothed. Our spirit doesn't become inflamed, but it does need to feel peaceful or experience a sense of wonder and awe.

Immunity

Understanding, love and compassion buffer us from any craziness or cruelty circling around. We may understand but are not harmed by any of it. Just as we need to boost our immune system against stray viruses in the fall, we need to boost our mental and emotional capacity to be discerning with respect to the quantities of information and disinformation bombarding us. And we need to be strong, loving and aware when dealing with our emotional issues and those of others.

These forms of immunity ensure that we are not triggered or sucked back into the void of trauma, and we can lead a healthy, balanced life and thrive.

Sit comfortably and breathe deeply, rhythmically and gently. As before, consider the holistic model and apply the same scale of 0 (bad) to 10 (excellent) to the following questions. Answer quickly and honestly.

- ✧ How strong is my immunity generally?

  ____

- ✧ How immune is my mind to untruth?

  ____

- ✧ How immune is my body to viruses?

  ____

- ✧ How immune are my emotions to manipulation?

  ____

- ✧ How strong is my spirit?

  ____

Ideally, you want your answers to be over 6. If any of your answers fall below 5, please look for information, strategies, and tips to follow to reinforce your immunity. Immunity is not disinterest. It is the ability to stand in strength and integrity, to be discerning and resistant to outside negativity.

Summary

Our inner lives do not follow a straight line. Research shows that our cells hold our emotions. When we are healing trauma, we need to listen to our bodies as well as our minds, emotions, spirit and energy to assess how we are progressing. This chapter provides you with easy ways to check in, adjust and rebalance on a regular basis.

We know that we have moved outside the vortex of trauma the moment we look back on the event without feeling traumatized. We may feel sad, we may know that we will never be the same, nor will our lives, but we no longer feel pulled back by the past, unable to move forward. We are no longer victims.

At a very deep level, we have changed more profoundly than we would have believed possible. We have found inner peace as we move forward with courage, compassion and love, now guided by a different star.

APPENDIX 1

The Stress Response: Stress Impacts the Whole Body

Stress is considered to be the first stage of, or trigger for, nearly every illness. To understand why, it is necessary to recognize what happens within our bodies when we activate the fight, flight or freeze response. Listed below are some of the physical changes that can occur as a result of extreme danger or stress. From this list, it is easy to understand why stress can be considered deadly.

The Stress Response

- Cortisol is released from the adrenal glands to protect us from an instant allergic reaction, such as breathing difficulties caused by dust, pollen or air pollution. If chronically elevated, cortisol destroys the body's resistance to the stresses of cancer, infection, surgery and illness; the lymph glands shrivel up, and the

STRESS IMPACTS THE WHOLE BODY

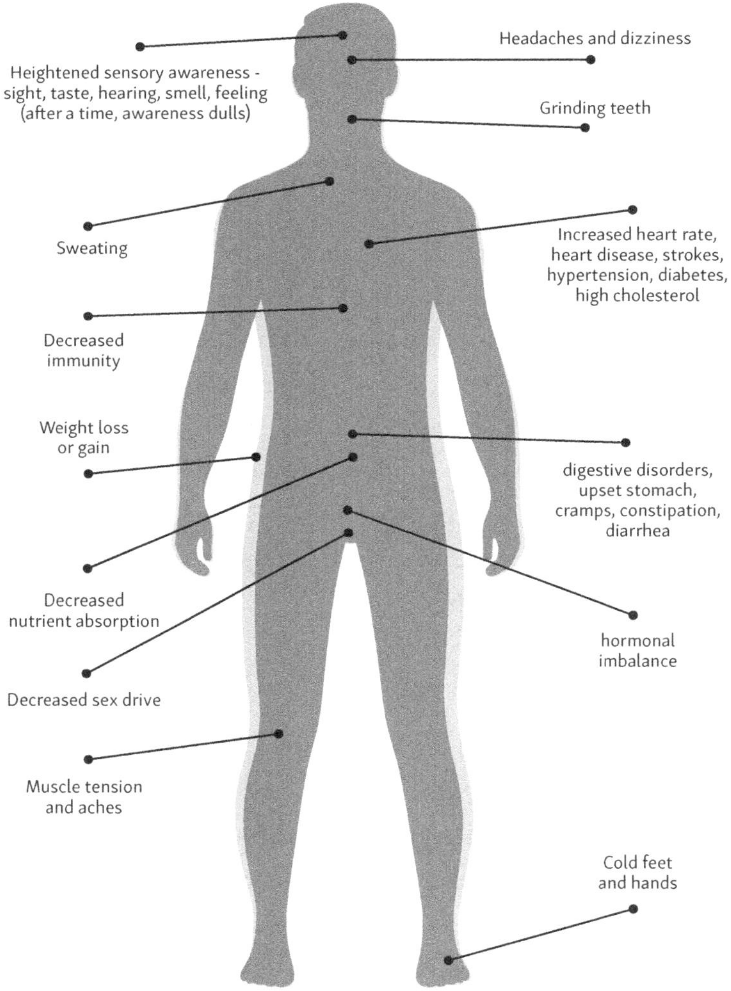

Examples of how stress affects the body.

Originally printed in *Let Stress Heal Your Life: Uncover Your Amazing Capacity to Thrive* by Gillian Padgett. Vernon, BC: SWS Publishing (2017). Used with permission.

immune system weakens. (See appendix 2)

- Thyroid hormones increase in the bloodstream to speed up the metabolism in order to produce extra energy. If left unchecked, this increase can cause intolerance to heat, shaky nerves, jumpiness, insomnia, exhaustion, burnout and weight loss.
- Endorphins released from the hypothalamus are feel-good hormones and a powerful pain-killer. Chronic stress depletes endorphin levels and has been shown to aggravate migraines, backaches and the pain of arthritis.
- The digestive tract shuts down, and blood is diverted to the muscles, heart and lungs. The mouth becomes dry, the stomach bloats and cramps occur. General discomfort, nausea, diarrhea and difficulties with elimination of bladder and bowels may occur.
- Sugar is released into the blood as a quick energy supply—fuel for the sprint—along with increased insulin to metabolize it. Diabetes can be aggravated or even started by excessive demands on the pancreas for insulin. Eating sugary foods when the body is already creating its own sugar can result in hyperglycemia.

- Cholesterol in the blood, mainly from the liver, increases, which helps provide long-distance fuel now that the stomach has shut down. Cholesterol takes over where blood sugar leaves off in supplying energy to the muscles. This can cause hardening of the arteries and fatal heart attacks. In times of extreme stress, cholesterol levels can rise by 40 percent.
- A racing heartbeat carries more blood to the muscles and lungs to provide extra oxygen where it is needed, which can result in high blood pressure, strokes and fatal heart attacks. Feet and hands feel cold.
- An increased air supply provides extra oxygen to feed the increased blood supply coming into the lungs. The nostrils flare, the throat dilates, all of the air passages to the lungs dilate and breathing becomes more rapid. This is particularly difficult for smokers, who often smoke more when under stress.
- The blood thickens to fight infections, carry more oxygen and stop bleeding. This thickening can increase the risk of strokes and heart attacks.

- The skin crawls, pales and sweats. It crawls because the skin's tiny hairs stand on end; it pales as blood is diverted to the heart, lungs and muscles and away from any cuts; and it sweats to keep the muscles cool.
- All five senses become acute to provide peak physical activity, appropriate reactions and increased concentration.
  - The pupils dilate, resulting in improved night and peripheral vision.
  - Our hearing becomes acute, and
  - Our senses of touch, taste and smell become enhanced.

After experiencing excessive stress, our senses become duller, putting us at risk for making dangerous moves and choices—for example, when driving.

APPENDIX 2
Fear Triggers the Stress Response in the Body

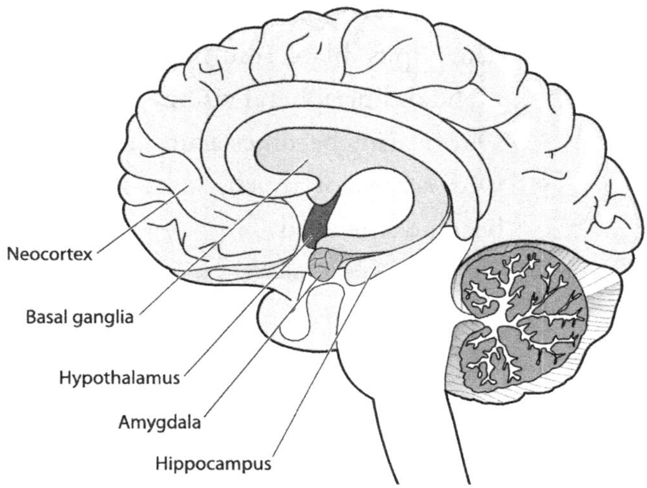

The Amygdala is responsive to fear. It turns on the stress response and triggers the release of adrenaline and cortisol secretion.

Originally printed in *Let Stress Heal Your Life: Uncover Your Amazing Capacity to Thrive* by Gillian Padgett. Vernon, BC: SWS Publishing (2017). Used with permission.

APPENDIX 3
The Interconnectedness of Mind, Body, Emotions and Spirit

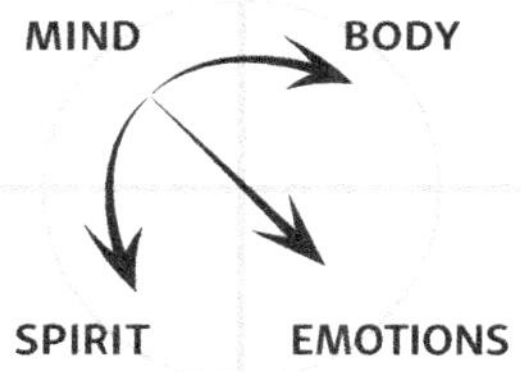

MIND (M)
Mental stress can affect the body, emotions and spirit

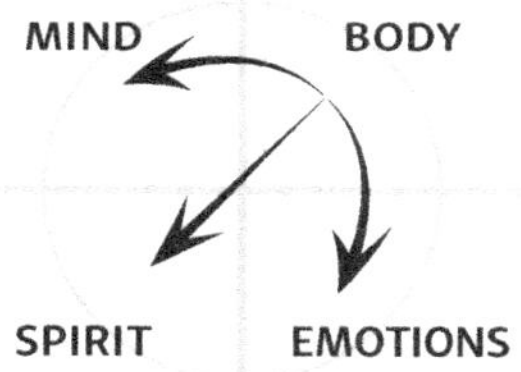

BODY (B)
Physical stress can affect the mind, emotions and spirit

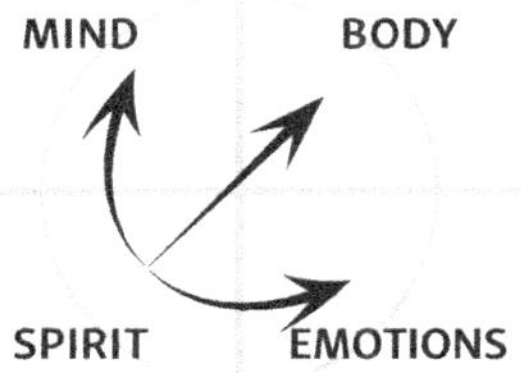

SPIRIT (S)
Spiritual stress can affect the mind, body and emotions
Note: The spirit refers to an inner sense of joy and energy for life.

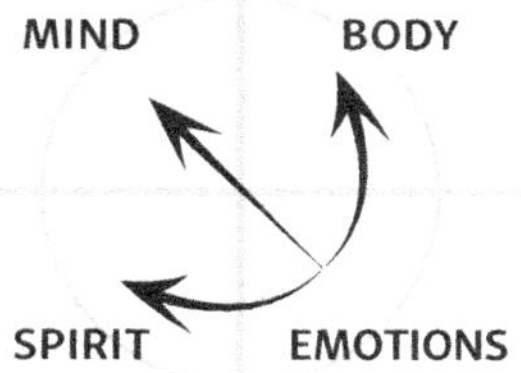

EMOTIONS (E)
Emotional stress can affect the mind, body and spirit

> When stress affects one area of our being (MBES), it also touches and affects other areas (MBES) and influences overall wellbeing, whether or not we are conscious of this taking place at the time. Likewise, positive experiences, feelings and actions can touch one area, affect other areas and influence overall wellbeing.

Originally printed in *Let Stress Heal Your Life: Uncover Your Amazing Capacity to Thrive* by Gillian Padgett. Vernon, BC: SWS Publishing (2017). Used with permission.

APPENDIX 4
The Left and Right Hemispheres of the Brain

THE BRAIN

LEFT BRAIN

Controls right side of the body
Number skills
Math/scientific skills
Written language
Objectivity
Analytical
Logic
Reasoning

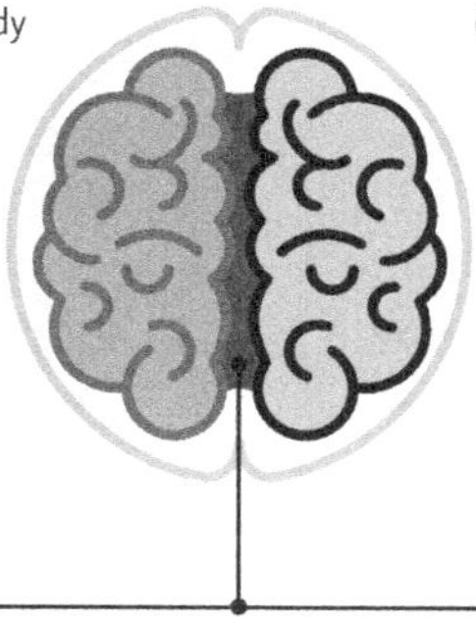

RIGHT BRAIN

Controls left side of the body
3D shapes
Music/Art awareness
Intuition
Subjectivity
Emotions
Creativity/imagination
Face recognition

THE CORPUS CALLOSUM

The corpus callosum Is a bundle of nerve fibers that connects and facilitates the communication between the left and right sides of the brain.

Originally printed in *Let Stress Heal Your Life: Uncover Your Amazing Capacity to Thrive* by Gillian Padgett. Vernon, BC: SWS Publishing (2017). Used with permission.

Resources

Believe nothing,
No matter where you read it or who has said it,
Not even if I have said it,
Unless it agrees with your own reason
And your own common sense.
Buddha

There is a wealth of information to be found on the internet related to stress, trauma, health and well-being, as well as a continuing flow of books and specialist publications on the topics.

Listed below are some of my favourite books related to mental, emotional, physical and spiritual well-being, stress and trauma. Some of them may be available only in the library. Their wisdom is timeless.

Discernment is Recommended

Money now plays a disproportionate role whether related to the food we consume, the supplements or medications we are prescribed or the services and support we may be considering. Many are promoted before proven to be safe, healthy or effective and may eventually be found to be harmful, while others are discredited despite a history of therapeutic success. It is up to us to do our own research, be cautious and discerning when making choices that are likely to be least harmful and most healthful.

Achterberg, Jeanne & Associates. *Rituals of Healing: Using Imagery for Health and Wellness*: Bantam Books, 1994.

Anderson, Bob. *Stretching*. CA: Shelter Publications, 2000.

Axline, Virginia. *Dibs in Search of Self: The Moving Story of an Emotionally Lost Child Who Found His Way Back*: Penguin Books, 1983.

Bollinger, Ty. *The Truth about Cancer: What You Need to Know About Cancer's History, Treatment, and Prevention*. Carlsbad, CA: Hay House, 2016.

Braden, Gregg. *The Turning Point: Creating Resilience in a Time of Extremes*. Carlsbad, CA: Hay House, 2014.

Braden, Gregg. *The Spontaneous Healing of Belief: Shattering the Paradigm of False Limits*. Carlsbad, CA: Hay House, 2008.

Braden, Gregg. *Secrets of the Lost Mode of Prayer: The Hidden Power of Beauty, Blessing, Wisdom and Hurt*. Carlsbad, CA: Hay House, 2006.

Buscaglia, Leo. *Living, Loving & Learning*. New York: Ballantine, 1982.

Campbell, T. Colin, and Thomas M. Campbell. *The China Study: Startling Implications for Diet, Weight Loss and Long-term Health*. Dallas, TX: Benbella Books, 2006.

Carr, Kris. *Crazy Sexy Diet: Eat Your Veggies, Ignite Your Spark and Live Like You Mean It!* Guildford, CT: Skirt! Global Pequot Press, 2011.

Carr, Kris. *Crazy Sexy Juice: 100+ simple juice, smoothie & nut milk recipes to supercharge your health*. Carlsbad, CA: Hay House, 2015.

Chopra, Deepak. *Quantum Healing: Exploring the Frontiers of Mind/Body Medicine*. New York: Bantam Books, 1989.

Chopra, Deepak. *You Are the Universe: Discovering Your Cosmic Self and Why it Matters*. USA: Harmony Books, 2017.

Cousins, Norman. *Anatomy of an Illness*. New York: Bantam Books, 1981.

Dispenza, Joe. *You Are the Placebo: Making Your Mind Matter*. Carlsbad, CA: Hay House, 2014.

Dispenza, Joe. *Breaking the Habit of Being Yourself: How*

to Lose Your Mind and Create a New One. Carlsbad, CA: Hay House, 2012.

Dispenza, Joe. *Evolve Your Brain: The Science of Changing Your Mind*. Deerfield Beach, FL: Health Communications, 2007.

Doidge, Norman. *The Brain's Way of Healing: Remarkable Discoveries and Recoveries from the Frontiers of Neuroplasticity*. New York: Penguin Books, 2015.

Dossey, Larry. *Healing Words: The Power of Prayer and the Practice of Medicine*. Harper One, 1993.

Emoto, Masaru. *The Healing Power of Water*. Carlsbad, CA: Hay House, 2004.

Enders, Giulia. *Gut: The Inside Story of Our Body's Most Underrated Organ*. Greystone Books, 2015.

Gach, Michael Reed. *Acupressure's Potent Points: A Guide to Self-Care for Common Ailments*. New York: Bantam Books, 1990.

HeartMath Institute. https://www.heartmath.com/institute-of-heartmath.

Levine, Peter. *Healing Trauma: A Pioneering Program for Restoring the Wisdom of Your Body*. Boulder, CO: Sounds True, 2005.

Lipton, Bruce. *The Biology of Belief: Unleashing the Power of Consciousness, Matter & Miracles*. Carlsbad, CA: Hay House, 2008.

Lipton, Bruce. *The Honeymoon Effect: The Science of Creating Heaven on Earth*. Carlsbad, CA: Hay House, 2013.

Marchant, Jo. *A Journey into the Science of Mind Over*

Body. New York: Crown Publishers, 2016.

Mate, Gabor. *When the Body Says NO: The Cost of Hidden Stress*. Toronto, ON: Random House, 2003.

Mazo, Ellen. *The Immune Advantage: How to Boost Your Immune System: The Single Most Important Thing You Can Do for Your Health*. London: Rodale Limited, 2004.

McGonigal, Kelly. *The Upside of Stress: Why Stress is Good for You and How to Get Good at it*. New York: Avery Penguin Random House, 2015.

Nakazawa, Donna Jackson. *Childhood Disrupted: How Your Biography Becomes Your Biology and How You Can Heal*. New York: Atria, 2015.

Perlmutter, David, and Alberto Villoldo. *Power up Your Brain: The Neuroscience of Enlightenment*. Carlsbad, CA: Hay House, 2011.

Pert, Candace. *Molecules of Emotion: The Science of Mind-Body Medicine*. New York: Touchstone, 1999.

Rankin, Lissa. *Mind Over Medicine: Scientific Proof That You Can Heal Yourself*. Carlsbad, CA: Hay House, 2013.

Rankin, Lissa. *The Fear Cure: Cultivating Courage as Medicine for the Body, Mind and Soul*. Carlsbad, CA: Hay House, 2014.

Robbins, Ocean, and John Robbins. The Food Revolution Network. https://foodrevolution.org.

Shealy, C. Normal. *The Illustrated Encyclopedia of Healing Remedies*. Shaftesbury, Dorset, UK: Element Books, 1998.

Sitt, Barbara Reed. *Food & Behavior: A Natural Connection*. Manitowoc, WI: Natural Press, 2004.

Tolle, Eckhart. *The Power of Now.* Vancouver, BC: Namaste Publishing, 1997.

I recommend reading the central spiritual books for all the religions (or summaries of them).

GRATITUDE

THANK YOU!

June Burrough: Your gift of friendship and our lengthy long-distance calls have helped to keep me on track. I so admire your courage and spirit as you take on and move through extraordinary challenges to manifest your beautiful dreams.

Wendy Gilbert: Thank you for your friendship and for always being able to answer my tech questions and bring back to life frozen or disappeared documents.

Bill Harrison: I am so grateful to you for recommending that I write a short book on trauma. It took a little longer to materialize than the two or three weeks suggested and imagined, but I am certain the topic is perfect for this moment in time.

Chris Padgett: I am boundlessly grateful to you for patiently going through the entire edited manuscript with me during your visit for my birthday. The program was utterly confusing to me and you made it seem so simple.

Heidi Reid: I deeply appreciate your support and encouragement and for believing in me and the path I am on.

All my clients: Thank you for trusting me with your secrets and dreams and for allowing me to support you on your journey. I have learnt so much from you about courage, love and healing. It has been a delight and an absolute honor to work with you.

Everyone at Quantum Leap: Thank you for your guidance, patience, support and limitless resources.

I send you all love and deep gratitude.

About the Author

Gillian Padgett has always enjoyed helping people through her work as an interior designer, hypnotherapist and psychotherapist. After the murder of her best friend and witnessing the devastation to her friend's family, Gillian pursued training to work with victims of crime and families of murder victims in the UK. This led her to study stress and well-being from as many perspectives as she could find. Stress then became the focus of her work.

It is now known that poorly managed stress is the foundation of most illnesses. This is reason enough to understand stress and trauma; know how to nourish and nurture ourselves; be able to maintain balance between mind, body, emotions and spirit; effectively handle whatever comes our way on our journey through life; and be able to cope with trauma, relieve stress and be stress resilient. Sharing this information has become Gillian's life purpose, through her books, online programs and with clients.

From Trauma to Tranquility: A Guide to Inner Peace is designed as a guide, to understand the impact of trauma, remove fear and provide strategies and steps to move through trauma in your own way, at your own pace and to reach a new sense of ease, wisdom and inner peace.

Gillian's previous book *Let Stress Heal Your Life: Uncover Your Amazing Capacity to Thrive* includes guidelines and practical, proven ways to successfully relieve stress and become stress resilient no matter what is going on around you.

Visit her website, www.gillianpadgett.com, to learn more about Gillian's books, resources and services.

Relaxation for Trauma Relief
has been designed and recorded
by the author to accompany this book.
The MP3 is available free on the link below:
www.stresswisdomsolutions.com/fttt

Made in the USA
Monee, IL
04 November 2026

67382363R00075